Exploring the Dundas Valley

Cameron Goede

Exploring the Dundas Valley

Cameron Goede

ISBN 978-1518637780

All photography is by the author unless noted as otherwise.

Front cover image by John Michael Goede

Rear cover image by Lisa Mark Photography

Printed in the United States of America

For Sally, Julia, John and Liam, the best family I could ever imagine.

Acknowledgments

Numerous people were instrumental in the book becoming a reality, most notably my family. My wife Sally has been my biggest advocate, providing encouragement, proof reading services and a high level of support as I embarked on this project. My children as well have provided endless support, often joining me on hikes or sharing tales of their own experiences exploring the valley. All three; Julia, John and Liam have inherited their own love of nature and the outdoors which is something that I am eternally grateful for. My brother Ryan Goede who also joins me on the trails has provided endless inspiration and ideas and I'm grateful for his company.

Many of my adventures have been shared with a canine companion as I have often found that exploring the trails alone but with a faithful dog at my side adds another wonderful component to the experience. My first dog Rosie spent more hours than I can count wandering trails through all kinds of weather and always was excited to see the hiking gear coming out of the closet. She was a permanent sidekick on many of our adventures until her passing in 2013.

My second dog Stella, a rescue dog with a huge heart has been my trail companion ever since and we continue to explore and enjoy the valley at every opportunity.

I would like to acknowledge my friend Steve Parton, without whose encouragement and insight, this book would never have been completed.

A note of appreciation to Ryan Goede and Frances Maas who graciously supplied photos in areas where I needed them.

Special thanks also go to the Hamilton Conservation Authority and the Royal Botanical Gardens for their tireless work in preserving this area for future generations.

Introduction

Keep close to Nature's heart... and break clear away, once in a while, and climb a mountain or spend a week in the woods. Wash your spirit clean. – John Muir

With its peaks, vistas, waterfalls and vast trail system, the Dundas Valley and surrounding area offer some of the most varied and accessible opportunities for outdoor activity in southern Ontario. Living in the area, I quickly developed a deep love of the valley and continue to spend much of my time here.

I would often be asked for ideas and suggestions of areas to explore and as result, my blog on the Dundas Valley was born. I looked upon it as an opportunity to share my stories and my photos and to provide a service to those who were interested in learning more. It was truly a labour of love.

Sell your books at sellbackyourBook.com!
Go to sellbackyourBook.com and get an instant price quote. We even pay the shipping - see what your old books are worth today!

00052325380

0005232 **5380** S

As blog posts were written and shared, the inevitable comments and dialogue ensued and within a few years the early idea of a book started to hatch. My vision was this; develop a resource that could provide would-be visitors with a guide for hiking and exploring and a way to perhaps find areas that they may have otherwise not known were there. I knew that there were stories to share, fascinating historical facts to explore and secret trails and destinations that couldn't be found through other publications.

I envisioned something that was part picture book, part trail guide and part story telling.

What you are holding is the culmination of that vision. I thank you for taking the time to read it and for sharing my passion. I hope that you find it interesting and informative and if new to the area, perhaps the catalyst to drive you to explore this area more. I am sure that you will quickly become enamored with its beauty, as I have.

Happy exploring!

Table of Contents

A Wander in the Woods

Today I wandered.

With some time to myself and no clear destination in mind, I headed into the valley and was quickly enveloped by the quietness of the forest now freshly covered in snow.

I let my puppy companion determine the direction and based on her whim and the scents that caught her attention we followed the Spring Creek Trail. At various points we paused to admire the creek as its open water and frozen sections intertwined creating random patterns of light and dark. We would stop and then continue to wander.

Deer tracks crossed over the trail at many points, an indication of the large number of them that call this section of the valley home. At one point a red tailed hawk caught our attention as it flew from tree to tree like a sentinel announcing our presence. The trees were alive with other birds as well, mostly cardinals and woodpeckers and we stopped to watch them too. We would enjoy for a minute and then, you guessed it, continue to wander.

That's the great thing about wandering without a clear destination in mind; we had the time to stop and take in each view as well as change direction whenever we wanted.

At some point I was reminded of the Henry David Thoreau quote: "The scenery, when it is truly seen, reacts on the life of the seer. How to live. How to get the most of life... How to extract its honey from the flower of the world."

I stopped and pondered those words, smiled, and feeling like I had gained some new understanding, continued my wander.

Trails

The Dundas Valley and surrounding area contains within it many trails, rolling meadows, stunning vistas and beautiful waterfalls. From the easy walking flat gravel of the Hamilton to Brantford Rail Trail to the tricky and more technical terrain of the Spencer Gorge, there is something for every hiking level. The next 15 chapters explore these in depth. In each chapter you will find details related to location, hiking distance and

difficulty as well as relevant points of interest. Each of these trails is perfect for an afternoon and the close proximity of each makes the possibility of combining two or more of them in a day easy to accomplish.

Most of these trails are also mountain bike friendly and the area boasts a large cycling community. Be aware that in the early spring many of the trails are off limits to cycling and equestrian activity but these restrictions are lifted once the trail conditions firm up.

By all means, these routes that I describe do not include every possible trail in the area as doing so would require a much more ambitious endeavor than this book. Consider the following as perhaps a list of the most known trails or at the very least, my personal favourites.

Fall Hiking on the Spring Creek Trail

"Listen, the wind is rising, and the air is wild with leaves. We have had our summer evenings, now for October eves."

- Humbert Wolfe

Although there is no bad time to be hiking in the Dundas Valley, there is something special about the fall. Cool clean air, the lack of bugs and distinctive crunch of leaves underfoot always remind me that another summer has come to an end and that the days of winter are not far away.

A popular hiking start point in the Dundas Valley is the Trail Centre. This centre is a replica of a Victorian train station from a bygone era and even features a section of track with a 1929 executive coach car and a 1931 baggage car that were donated by the Canadian Pacific Railway. Always popular with the kids, it's worth a visit.

The Trail Centre features a snack bar and interpretive displays and often features the artwork of local artists and photographers. Trail maps can be obtained there and being centrally located, it is a good launch point from which to explore various parts of the valley.

The Spring Creek Trail which is just over 3 km in length starts at the Trail Centre, follows the Spring Creek valley eastward, crosses Sanctuary Park and ends at Warren Park. Following this route you have the opportunity to walk through sun-dappled Carolinian groves with an elevated view of Spring Creek below. Frequently you can be entertained by the sight of deer peacefully grazing or spot raccoons, chipmunks and red or black squirrels busily going about their tasks. At times the forest changes to sumac and to marshland heavily populated with red-winged blackbirds and other song birds. Often times on this trail we spot wild turkeys, various varieties of snakes and woodpeckers.

As one of my favorites, the Spring Creek Trail often becomes my default route when I feel the need to get in the valley but am limited for time.

The Dundas Valley Trail Centre is located at 650 Governors Road in Dundas. There is plenty of parking. An entry fee is required at this location.

Dundas Valley – Main Loop

Probably the most common trail visited in the Dundas Valley, the Main Loop provides the hiker with exposure to a great many views and points of interest along its path.

This hilly trail starts and ends at the Dundas Valley Trail Centre and is just under 4 km in length. Along its path you will travel through mature deciduous forests and hemlock groves and see such landmarks as the Hermitage ruins as well as an old apple orchard, cold water streams and stunning geological formations.

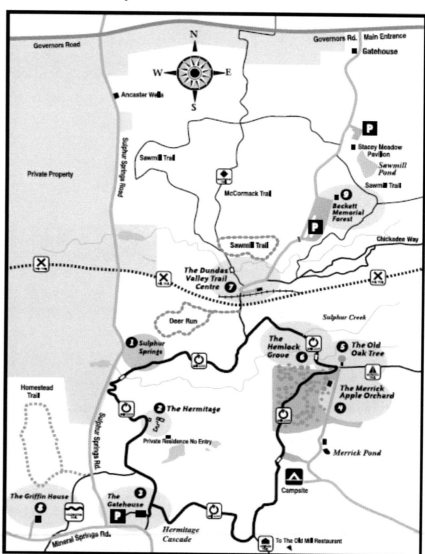

This area is home to a wide array of wildlife including rare animals, birds and plant life.

Travel through the old orchard and you will come upon a stately white oak tree. At over 150 years old, this silent sentry stands guard over the valley and provides a shady spot to rest. This is a great spot to watch for the red tail hawks, turkey vultures and numerous songbirds that call this area home.

Returning back to the Trail Centre, it's a perfect spot to enjoy a hot chocolate, view the displays and artwork in the centre and reflect on the views and enjoyable experiences of the day.

"In all things of nature, there is something of the marvelous." Aristotle

Spring Creek – Sawmill Trail Loop

Last Saturday morning I was looking to hit a trail both as a cardio workout as well as to test out a new pedometer app that I had added to my phone. Staying close to home, I decided that I would hike the Spring Creek Trail to the Trail Centre and then return a different way, creating sort of a loop. This turned out to be a good idea from a workout standpoint as well as an opportunity to enjoy some beautiful parts of the Dundas Valley.

You can start this hike at the end of Bridlewood Drive in Dundas, entering the valley on the well-marked trail and heading west. The Spring Creek Trail like the name insinuates, follows the meandering Spring Creek and runs roughly parallel to the

Hamilton to Brantford Rail Trail. You pass a pond that I often stop at to watch frogs and birds and then pass through hilly Carolinian forest. This is a great spot to observe deer particularly if you hike in the early morning or late afternoon. On this day I was able to get within 15 feet of a pair of them as they grazed and even with my dog at my side they did not seem particularly concerned with my presence.

Stopping at the Trail Centre for some water we started heading back in the direction we came but veering left when we got to the marker for the Sawmill Trail. This trail takes you through milkweed filled meadows interspersed with black walnut trees and then directs you deeper into the valley. The key is to stay to your right as side trails branch off at various points. It was noticeably cooler as we walked along the creek edge and I enjoyed how complete the silence was; only broken by the song of the various finches and chickadees that flitted in and out of the sumac trees.

This trail ends at the John White Trail. Turning right and crossing a wooden footbridge, you soon arrive back on the Spring Creek Trail. Head east and you will arrive back at the starting point in about 15 minutes. Other than my pedometer app stopping at some point likely due to being in a low area with no cell service, this was a very enjoyable walk. At approximately 3 miles, it took me just over an hour but that included stopping to take photos and letting my dog play in the water.

McCormack Trail

Minus 14 degrees Celsius and sunny, a perfect morning for exploring. Under an impossibly blue sky my dog and I headed up the trail from Governors Road on the farm laneway that makes up the first section of the trail. Passing the meadows of Valley Farms, a few horses were grazing and seemed oblivious to our passing.

Within a few minutes we arrived at the pond. This is a spot that I frequently hike to in the summer as it is common to see wood ducks, mallards and the occasional blue heron here. On this day, with the pond frozen over, all was silent.

Leaving the pond we continued north. There are a couple of trails branching off to the right that will take you through the meadow and uphill. I have hiked there many times and the view from the top is pretty neat with views clear to Cootes Paradise and the city of Hamilton.

This day we continued down the trail, hitting a steep downhill section and reaching a fork in the path. We chose to turn left for no other reason than my dog, following a scent, decided she wanted to go that way. Heading west the trail wound through a forest of maple and oak and then turned back to meadow as it circled back towards the direction from where we had come. This is essentially a large loop taking you back through grazing pasture towards Valley Farm. As this trail winds through active pasture please be respectful of the gates, ensuring that they remain closed. There are frequently horses in this area so it is also important to ensure that if you bring your dog, they remain on the leash.

Connecting back to the main trail, we paused at the fence overlooking the farm and a few of the horses came over to greet us.

This trail is picturesque and well worth hiking. It remains relatively unknown and always seems to be very quiet. It certainly gets my recommendation if you are looking for an easy short hike with great views.

The McCormack Trail entrance is located on Governors Road almost directly across the road of the main entrance to the Dundas Valley Conservation Area.

Bruce Trail – Sherman Falls to Canterbury Falls

A great example of a trail with easy access is the trail that runs from Sherman Falls to Canterbury Falls. This trail, part of the Bruce Trail system, has plenty of road side parking and provides lots of beautiful views.

To access, drive down Old Dundas Road and park where the road meets Lions Club Road. From here you can already see the beautiful 17 metre (56 ft) high Sherman Falls through the trees and within a couple of minutes you will be standing at the base of the waterfall. Particularly in the spring or after a rain, the waterfall typically has a strong flow.

After taking in this amazing view continue on and follow the trail back downstream, but now on the other side of the stream. Follow the trail up the steep rock and you will soon be at the top of the rocky escarpment and walking through the woods deeper into the Canterbury Hills area. This area changes so much with the seasons and so on this day as I took photos I noted that everything was turning green and spring flowers were coming into bloom. The wildlife was also very active.

Hearing a noise to my left I stopped and stood motionless as a group of a dozen deer entered a clearing beside me. They stopped to graze, looking up anytime I made even the slightest movement or sound but continued to move closer to where I stood. Eventually when they were about 20 feet away and I am sure hearing the sound of the shutter on my camera, they ventured off, looking behind periodically to be sure I wasn't following. It is scenes such as these that keep me coming back and exploring these trails at every opportunity.

Within a few minutes I came upon this young raccoon climbing a tree. Although he was nearly 25 feet off the ground, the raised trail that I was on put us directly in front of each other. We stared at each other for a few minutes and as I didn't want to add any stress to him I continued walking, after taking a few photos of course.

Rounding a bend I approached Canterbury Falls. The Canterbury Falls area really has two waterfalls, both of them being fed by a tributary of Sulphur Creek which is also sometimes referred to as Canterbury Creek. On this day, Little Canterbury Falls, a 5 metre (16 ft) tall ribbon cascade was almost dry with just a trickle of water flowing.

The second and larger of the two is Canterbury Falls which is a 9.5 metre (31 ft) high terraced ribbon cascade with a crest width of 3.3 metres (11 ft). It features a wooden footbridge across the creek right at the crest of this waterfall and on this day the water was flowing nicely.

Ray Lowes Side Trail – Borer's Falls

Parking at the small lot on York Road I headed down the Ray Lowes Side Trail and into the valley. It was a cool slightly foggy November morning, perfect for hiking and the trails were empty with the exception of my dog and I. Our destination: Borer's Falls.

The trail very quickly wound downwards into the valley and with most of the leaves now down, the view was open and beautiful. As the trail begins the climb up the escarpment the scenery changes to moss covered rocky outcroppings and stands of birch.

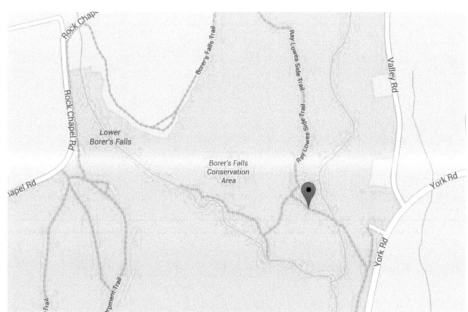

This area also provides a habitat for many significant species of plants and animals including the largest single population in Canada of Red Mulberry, a nationally endangered tree species.

At the top of the climb there are stairs that have been cut into the rock that provide a close up view of the layered sedimentary rock that makes up the escarpment. Once at the top this trail links up with the famous Bruce Trail.

By the time we reached the top the sun had burnt off the last of the fog and the view across the valley was spectacular.

Continuing along the escarpment edge, there are plenty of spots that provide clear vantage points of the valley below and the amazing eastern white cedars that cling unbelievably to the cliff-edge. The trail winds past farm fields and as it starts to approach the falls the unmistakable sound of rushing water gets louder.

Borer's Falls is a classical, 17 metre (56 ft) waterfall, also known as Rock Chapel Falls. It is considered is a true plunge waterfall as the water does not make contact with the bedrock until it reaches the base of the falls.

The waterfalls once powered the Rock Chapel village sawmill which was run by the Borer family for more than 100 years. Land clearing in the area eventually altered the creek's flow to such an extent that it could no longer provide sufficient energy so the family switched to steam to power the mill.

There are many spots to view the falls including a bridge that provides a stunning view of the gorge.

This area is now managed by the Hamilton Conservation Authority and the Royal Botanical Gardens as a nature reserve. It provides a link between Cootes Paradise and the Niagara Escarpment and is host to a wide variety of plants and animals including large stands of lilacs.

On the hike back we paused to admire a historical old stone wall that harkened back to pioneer times and we observed countless red and black squirrels as well as a number of curious chipmunks as they scampered noisily over the fallen leaves.

This hike takes about 40 minutes each way and is rather hilly but well worth the effort. I always look forward to returning!

The Dundas Peak

The Dundas Peak is a popular hiking destination and probably one of the best known Dundas outdoor attractions. Lofty in height and overlooking the valley town with changing seasonal colours, it serves as a permanent symbol of the escarpment that helps to make Dundas such a unique place. It also signals the entryway to the Spencer Gorge.

The Spencer Gorge Wilderness Area is part of the Niagara Escarpment and has been declared by the United Nations (UNESCO) as a World Biosphere Reserve. This unique geological formation contains a few of Hamilton's best waterfalls, one of its best lookouts and hundreds of species of wildlife living in this Carolinian forest.

The most common route to get to the peak is by parking at Tew's Falls Conservation Area which is located on Harvest Road in Greensville. From there the well-marked trail takes you to two different look-out points that provide views of the spectacular 41 metre (134 ft) waterfall and then proceeds along the gorge perimeter.

This trail although well-groomed is right on the edge of the gorge and at times the drop off beside it is sheer. It is important to stay alert and watch your footing. At various points where the trail has narrowed there have been protective barriers placed to aid in hiker safety. The views into the gorge below continually change and are amazing.

Arriving at the peak, the panoramic view is breathtaking. The view takes in the entire town of Dundas as well as provides a view of the rail line below and the entire Spencer Gorge. Beautiful anytime of the year, it is particularly stunning in the fall.

If you are looking to hike to this point but want to shorten the walk, consider this little known shortcut: Leave Dundas by going up the Sydenham hill, turn left on Fallsview Road and at the second curve you will see a trail going into the woods on your left side. There is room to park on the shoulder here and the trail that you follow will quickly connect to the main trail. Turn left at this point and you will reach the peak in about 20 minutes.

Spencer Gorge - Lower Tew's Falls and Webster's Falls

I am frequently asked what my favourite hiking trail in the Dundas Valley is. With the vast selection and a multitude of beautiful and interesting destinations here, you may think that this would be a tough question to answer but for me it's easy. In my mind the hike into the Spencer Gorge from the CN rail line to Webster's Falls has it all; stunning views, fast water, challenging trails and beautiful waterfalls.

Parking on Woodley Lane by the Dundas Golf and Curling Club, I followed the railway service entrance along the north side of the CN railway tracks and followed them in an eastern direction towards Spencer Creek. The trail I was looking for can be found just to the west side of the creek and it follows the western bank taking you north towards Webster's Falls. Please be extremely careful in this area. These railway tracks are active and there have been accidents in the past. Ensure that you walk leaving plenty of space between you and the tracks.

The Spencer Gorge Wilderness Area is part of the Niagara Escarpment, declared by the United Nations (UNESCO) as a World Biosphere Reserve. This unique geological formation contains a few of Hamilton's best waterfalls, one of its best lookouts and hundreds of species of wildlife living in this Carolinian forest.

This trail is quite technical with uneven rock-strewn areas, narrow sections with steep drop-offs and plenty of tree roots to navigate over. Boots with good traction are a must. The reward for your hard work is that the views are amazing and the area has a very rugged natural feel, much like you would experience hiking into more remote locations.

As the trail descends down towards the water level there are various spots where the water creates rapids as it shoots over and around the large moss covered rocks. One of my favourite places to stop is where Logies Creek empties into Spencer Creek. From this bank you can see Lower Tew's Falls through the trees.
Continuing along the trail there are a couple of spots where it becomes very narrow and care must be taken as there is a 25 foot drop to the rocky creek bed below. Once through this section the walk is easy and within a few minutes you can hear the rushing sound of the water coming over Webster's Falls. The view as you round the curve in the trail and first spot Webster's Falls is a great reward and well worth the effort made to get this far.

As you approach the rushing waters you will see a narrow waterfall on your left. This complex ribbon waterfall is called Baby Webster's Falls. At times the water flow here is very light and it is best seen immediately after a seasonal storm or after the winter snow melt. Its height is 9 metres (30 ft) and its width is 3 metres (10 ft).

Webster's Falls is always a sight to see and at 22 metres (72 ft) in height with a crest width about the same, it makes for an impressive photo opportunity.

Heading back out, look for a trail that takes you up the bank to your right. You will see the white markers indicating the Bruce Trail. This elevated trail is somewhat easier and provides great views of the creek below as well as the interesting stone formations of the canyon walls.

All in all, a great hike and one I always enjoy.

Spencer Gorge - Lower Tew's Falls and Tew's Falls

As a continuation of the previous chapter in which I referred to Spencer Gorge as "my favourite hiking trail in the Dundas Valley", this one ranks right up there too. Like the previous trail this one also contains many great views as well as some more physically demanding terrain.

Similar to hiking in to Webster's Falls, I again parked on Woodley Lane by the Dundas Golf and Curling Club, followed the railway service entrance along the north side of the CN railway tracks and continued in an easterly direction towards Spencer Creek. Again I must remind you that walking in the vicinity of railway tracks always carries with it some risks. Although there is plenty of space and it is easy to maintain a safe distance, care must be taken.

On this morning there seemed to be a lot of bird activity with a number of vultures lazily circling overhead and a group of robins darting in and out of the sumac trees that border the forest. I passed the entrance into the valley that I had taken the prior week, this time continuing to the eastern side of Spencer Creek before turning into the trees.

Image by Ryan Goede

Within seconds the train tracks were behind me and I was engulfed in the beauty of the Spencer Gorge Wilderness Area. The trail towards the falls is noted by white marks on some of the trees and as I traveled down this trail I had the swirling waters of Spencer Creek below me and the rocky walls of the gorge above me.

At the fork in the trail I headed downwards toward Lower Tew's Falls. Lower Tew's Falls is created near where Logies Creek empties into Spencer Creek and is a twin

curtain falls measuring 3.7 metres (12 ft) in height and 6.7 metres (22 ft) in width. Visiting this waterfall is a treat because there is some difficulty and effort required to get here and as a result is visited very infrequently. There is a remote feel to this location and I enjoy my visits here.

I continued upstream and after eventually rounding a bend, could see Tew's Falls ahead of me. The view from this angle was spectacular. This is a waterfall commonly viewed from the trails at the top of the canyon and to approach it from the bottom was something that I had wanted to do for some time. At 41 metres (134 ft) it is the highest waterfall in the Hamilton area and is only 12 metres (40 ft) shorter than Niagara Falls. Approaching it from downstream you can really appreciate just how tall it is and I spent quite a bit of time here just enjoying everything around me.

On the hike out I stopped to look at Ferguson Falls which unfortunately was almost completely dry due to the lack of winter runoff. This is one I need to come back for, perhaps after a good rain. While sitting and enjoying my coffee here I noticed this small snake that was in the rocks and damp earth near the base of these falls.

While walking the rail line back out I turned to admire the Dundas Peak above me, always impressive and again reminding me that there are many more trails here to explore.

The Spencer Creek Trail

As people travel up Cootes Drive heading out of Dundas many are unaware of how close they are to an interesting and wildlife rich trail. The Spencer Creek Trail starts at the corner of Cootes Drive and Dundas Street and runs along the shoreline of Spencer Creek. With wooded marshland on one side and Spencer Creek on the other, this trail provides a great opportunity to see song birds and other wildlife.

Crossing Cootes Drive, the trail enters the South Shore Trails of Cootes Paradise which is managed by the Royal Botanical Gardens. This trail continues to run between the West Pond and the shore of the creek leading you onto one of the largest river mouth wetland deltas on Lake Ontario. This area is a significant part of the Niagara Escarpment World Biosphere Reserve and is home to more than 750 native plant species, 277 types of migratory birds, 37 mammal species, 14 reptile species, 9 amphibian species and 68 species of fish.

On a recent December walk we observed many birds including a beautiful blue heron who consistently eluded my attempts to take his picture. At least the mallards were a little more cooperative.

As you walk deeper into this rich marshland, you can't help but notice how quiet it becomes and it amazes you that while so close to the city, this area remains tranquil and abundant in wildlife.

Although beautiful at any time of year, the late fall and early winter provide the opportunity to view areas normally hidden by lush vegetation, increasing the odds of viewing deer and other animals.

I headed back from the trail determined to visit again in the summer, this time by kayak or canoe as water travel would provide even greater opportunities to explore. The Cootes Paradise Marsh is definitely an area worth visiting. Parking is available at the trailhead close to the Canadian Tire Store in Dundas.

The Sydenham Falls Trail

"There's a waterfall where??"

That was my immediate reaction when my brother called me and asked how I felt about an early morning fall hike into Sydenham Falls. Even though I had lived in this area for over 20 years I was totally unaware that this waterfall existed.

That was quite a few years ago and now I make a point of hiking the Sydenham Falls trail at least once each season. The great thing about this trail is that it actually contains three waterfalls and if you visit when the runoff is heavier you will get a chance to view a fourth.

Often times in the past, I had seen the trail heading into the woods at the bottom of the Sydenham Hill, never realizing the beauty and interesting rock formations that would appear just steps beyond.

The first waterfall that you come upon is called Lower Sydenham Falls. It is approximately 4 metres (13 ft) high and is located below the railway bridge that crosses Sydenham Creek. There is a narrow wooden bridge that provides a good spot to view from and if you are feeling adventurous, a narrow and steep trail will take you to the water level.

As you continue up the trail about 100 metres, heading steadily uphill into the escarpment, you will find a side trail on your right with a very steep downhill grade. This somewhat treacherous descent will take you to the bottom of Middle Sydenham Falls. The climb is worth it as this 6 metre (20 ft) high washboard curtain falls is spectacular!

Heading back up the main trail you arrive at Upper Sydenham Falls which at approximately 14 metres (45 ft) tall is the largest of the three. It is a beautiful ribbon type falls and is a great spot to take photos.

Tucked between Middle and Upper Sydenham Falls you will see the fourth waterfall which is also beautiful but tends to dry up in the summer. This waterfall is called Lafarge Falls. This tall ribbon falls has water cascading down a rock face full of colour. On this day, December 31, 2011, we had just experienced a day of light rain which ensured that the falls was flowing well.

The easiest way to access this trail is through Cascades Park on Livingstone Drive in Dundas. I highly recommend this trail if you are looking to see a few waterfalls in a short span of time. Also, this trail features much uphill walking as you make your way up the escarpment so you get an additional cardio workout as a bonus!

Northshore Trail

One of my favourite Dundas trails particularly when I want to see birds is the Northshore Trail of the Royal Botanical Gardens. With mild temperatures this past weekend I decided to pay this diverse and interesting area a visit.

Heading down the Pinetum Trail we walked through stands of sumac and fir trees and soon linked up with the Bull's Point Trail. We decided to visit the Bull's Point lookout and on the way back veer down towards the water via the Marshwalk Trail.

The air was alive with the sounds of ducks and geese and we soon arrived at the wooden boardwalk that winds through the bulrushes and takes you to the lookout platform. From this vantage point you have a clear view of Rat Island and Cootes Paradise and the large variety of migratory waterfowl living here. Cootes Paradise Marsh is

41

considered one of the most important waterfowl staging habitats on the lower Great Lakes and the largest nursery habitat for fish in the region.

The trees along the shoreline were filled with chickadees, blue jays and cardinals and as we walked we spooked a group of five deer who bounded off ahead of us on the trail. The birds here are very friendly and if you are patient, will readily eat bird seed from your hand.

To visit the Northshore Trail park near the posted sign on York Road in Dundas. Just beyond the former parking lot a large map is posted that provides directions to each of the trails in this area.

Hamilton Brantford Rail Trail

As one of the trails that I frequent the most, the Hamilton Brantford Rail Trail provides a terrific avenue for walkers, runners and cyclists. As railroads have been abandoning their unused lines, progressive communities have turned them into multi-use trails for bicycling, hiking, and horseback riding.

There are actually two connecting trails, the West Hamilton-Jerseyville Trail maintained by the Hamilton Region Conservation Authority and the Jerseyville-Brantford Trail of the Grand River Conservation Authority. They are both excellent and together make for a continuous ride of about 40 km (25 miles).

The West Hamilton - Jerseyville Trail was the first to be constructed in 1993. It begins on the west side of Hamilton, near McMaster University, following the Dundas Valley for 18 km (11 miles) to the community of Jerseyville. The surface is a fine granular gravel. Past Jerseyville the trail is newer, having been constructed in 1996. The surface is of similar construction.

The trail weaves through an ever changing landscape. As you pass through and ascend out of the Dundas Valley the trail is enveloped with trees, opening periodically to afford spectacular views of meadows and forest. There are a number of side trails including the famous Bruce Trail that cross the Rail Trail offering plenty of opportunity to explore. The wildlife is plentiful with birds and deer.

Once out of the valley the trail is flat and the scenery is mostly farmland interspersed with small stands of forest. Here the trail is lightly travelled and very peaceful as you pass through the historic village of Jerseyville. As you get closer to Brantford the trail again passes through forest and crosses an old trestle bridge. It takes you back in time as you imagine steam locomotives travelling through the area hauling their wares.

The trail is well maintained with markers posted each kilometre from the Hamilton end and occasional benches are provided. Attractive plantings and signs have been installed at road crossings and a few parking lots have been constructed. Water, toilets and a snack bar are available at The Trail Centre in the Dundas Valley Conservation Area, about 6 km from the Hamilton end. The snack bar has limited hours and the indoor washrooms may also be closed at times. Water is available at an outside faucet near the trail. The centre provides interpretive information and a large scale map is posted there detailing the rail trail as well as the network of hiking trails in the area.

How to Find

At the Hamilton end the trail starts near the Fortinos grocery store at Ewen Road and Main Street. There are places to park at numerous spots along the trail wherever the trail passes a road. There is also parking and access from The Trail Centre in the Dundas Valley Conservation Area.

Crooks' Hollow Historical Trail

For a quick step back into time you don't have to travel far. Head up into the pretty hamlet of Greensville and onto Crooks' Hollow Road and you will soon see the entrance to the Crooks' Hollow Historical Trail.

Years ago this area used to feature a pretty lake, a reservoir created by the Crooks' Hollow Dam. When this dam aged beyond repair the decision was made to remove it and to re-naturalize the area. The results were spectacular. A trail now follows the bank of a winding Spencer Creek and a rustic looking steel bridge stands on the

site of the old dam. Birds and wildlife abound and the creek resembles what it might have looked like many years ago.

Crossing Crooks' Hollow Road, the ruins of the Darnley Grist Mill capture your attention immediately with their rough stone walls and remains of old window frames. A nearby plaque explains the history of the mill and standing there in its shadow you can't help but wonder what life must have been like, back in the day when water powered grinding wheels were used to process flour and grains. The Darnley Grist Mill  was constructed between 1811 and 1813. Originally the building was square and three stories high. A 9 metre (30 ft) high overshot waterwheel was mounted on the outside wall beside Spencer Creek. Water was drawn over the wheel to power the mill which housed four sets of grindstones used for feed and flour production.

Leaving the site of the mill and walking along the edge of the creek you quickly arrive at the Darnley Cascade. This 4 metre (13 ft) waterfall is formed as Spencer Creek drains from Christie Lake and heads towards the valley. An interesting fact is that, at 225 metres (738 ft) above sea level, the Darnley Cascade is the highest elevation waterfall in the Hamilton area.

Continuing along the trail the large and impressive Christie Dam Looms. This imposing structure was constructed beginning in 1970 and features a continuous walkway across the top, providing an excellent view of Christie Lake.

Christie Lake is one of the most picturesque lake settings on the Niagara Escarpment. Within its 336 hectares (830 acres) are 10 km (6 miles) of trails, a wildlife management area, wide open spaces, tall grass prairie meadows, forests and a beautiful 360 metre (1,181 ft) sand beach. Visitors can enjoy all that the great outdoors has to offer with canoeing, fishing, swimming, picnicking, hiking and even cross-country skiing when conditions permit.

The Crooks' Hollow Historical Trail is a beautiful trail that winds through pines and provides diverse and interesting scenery. It is certainly not as well-known as other parts of the Dundas Valley area but it is well worth a visit and is rich in natural beauty as well as history.

Autumn Hike at Christie Lake

Although any time is a good time to visit Christie Lake Conservation Area, autumn is particularly beautiful.

Getting there is easy with the main entrance located at 1000 Hwy 5 West in Dundas. The main trail follows the shoreline around the entire perimeter of the lake. This trail is well marked and takes you past stands of towering pines and sumac that at this time of year are ablaze in red.

As the trail approaches the northern point of the lake it becomes marshy and heavily populated with ducks and geese foraging among the bulrushes.

The best shoreline for viewing the fall colours is the eastern shore as it opens up along the beach. It provides clear views of the opposing shoreline and a good opportunity to take in the beauty of the changing leaves.

Hiking this trail at a relaxed pace will take approximately an hour and a half. With the changing seasons each visit takes on a different feel and you never know what you might see.

Christie Wildlife Area

The morning fog was just starting to lift as I headed down the trail at the Christie Wildlife Area. I had found this spot completely by accident, driving north on Middletown Road just north of Regional Road 8. Fortunately I had spotted the small parking lot on the left side of the road and now as luck would have it we were exploring a new trail.

This beautiful marsh area feeds into Christie Lake and features a relatively short and mostly flat perimeter trail that follows the shoreline of the marsh. I imagine that this area is teeming with wildlife during the spring and summer months but with it now being mid-November it was quiet with the exception of some song birds and a few groups of ducks, mostly mallards, occupying the water.

While exploring the trails we walked through stands of cedar and pine which transitioned into maple and other deciduous trees on the western shoreline. The trail is mostly grass covered and for the most part is clearly marked. It features a bridge where the trail begins the returning portion.

You can see by my GPS that I made one small error requiring me to backtrack when I realized I was off course but other than that the walk was enjoyable and quiet.

I made a mental note to definitely return as I would love to see the landscape during the winter, spring and summer seasons as well.

Discovering the Hendrie Valley

An area that is not directly a part of the Dundas Valley but is in very close proximity is the Hendrie Valley Trails of the Royal Botanical Gardens.

As a smaller scale version of Cootes Paradise this area includes the 100 hectare Grindstone Creek Valley and stretches to the end of Carroll's Bay. It contains the finest collection of floodplain wetlands on western Lake Ontario. Transferred to the Royal Botanical Gardens in 1941 for ecological protection, the area features slopes forested with old growth trees, a 60 hectare river mouth marsh complex and four creeks. Major access points are along Plains Road and include the RBG Centre and Cherry Hill Gate.

On a couple of occasions I have parked at the Cherry Hill Gate entrance which is located on Plains Road in Burlington but more typically I park at Valley Inn Road where it meets York Boulevard in Hamilton. This road is now closed to car traffic and provides a great way into this rich hiking area. There is also a small parking lot at the bottom of Spring Garden Road in Burlington, just past Woodland Cemetery. This lot is right by the water at Carroll's Bay and is in very close proximity to the marshland area and the mouth of Grindstone Creek. A popular meeting spot for photographers, this area is always teeming with birds. Herons, ospreys, hawks and a wide variety of waterfowl frequent this area and you will usually see groups of photographers equipped with the latest in equipment, working to capture these creatures in flight.

When walking this way you will cross under the railway bridge and find yourself in the Grindstone Marsh area. This is a great spot for birds and assorted waterfowl. You can see in this area that a large project is underway to create new banks along the water's edge and to provide a system that works as a natural barrier against invasive carp. This has been facilitated through the re-use of over 100,000 discarded and donated Christmas trees.

Following the trail through the Grindstone Creek Delta you soon arrive at a spectacular boardwalk that borders Grindstone Creek and provides an excellent vantage point to watch nesting birds and observe beaver and other wildlife. This is a perfect place to bird watch and if you bring some seed along you can have fun feeding the friendly birds by hand. Many of these birds will gladly pay you a visit and trade you the opportunity of a close up photo for a few sunflower seeds.

On recent walks I have seen many red-wing blackbirds, blue jays, cardinals and woodpeckers. With some luck you may also catch a glimpse of a fox or watch a group of beavers scavenging for brush in the bulrushes which surround the boardwalk.

Bruce Trail – Waterdown and Great Falls

Although outside of the Dundas Valley the close proximity of this trail and its beauty merit inclusion in this book. Located just minutes outside of Dundas, this section of the Bruce Trail winds through the Smokey Hollow Gorge in Waterdown, Ontario. This trail is, in a word, stunning and is definitely one worth checking out.

There is a small parking lot on Mill Street in Waterdown and a short trail takes you to a viewing platform that has been built right at the crest of Great Falls. The view of water rush over the falls and into the Smokey Hollow Gorge is beautiful. Great Falls, also known as Grindstone Falls, has a height of 10 metres (33 ft), and a crest width of 5 metres (16 ft).

Visiting now, few clues remain to suggest that this stream was once so large and powerful that it supplied numerous mills with the power needed to operate heavy machinery. As late as 1890 Smokey Hollow was the site of two large mills, 14 buildings, three houses and nine outbuildings. By 1912 however, the mills had all closed as the water level in Grindstone Creek had gone down and the steam engines that propelled the waterpower were believed to be too dangerous. Today, thanks to a rehabilitation program implemented by Waterdown residents, the locality is a beautiful and well-kept park.

As the Bruce Trail heads downstream of the falls the views continue to impress with rocky outcroppings and ever changing photo opportunities as Grindstone Creek cascades through and over massive boulders. Watch your step on this trail as you will experience many short ascents and  descents, many with steps and tricky tree roots to navigate over.

The park can be found on the Waterdown section of the Bruce Trail Map and guide books and is easy to get to when hiking the Bruce Trail.

If travelling by car drive along the 403 toward Toronto and exit on Hwy 6 North. Turn right on Hwy 5 (Dundas Street East). Head east and turn right on Mill Street. Keep driving until you come to Smokey Hollow Park on the right. Great Falls is close to the parking lot.

Waterfalls in Dundas

Dundas is blessed with an abundance of streams and waterfalls, all of which make for worthwhile hiking destinations. Quite a number of them offer excellent access with a few being more remote and requiring a little more effort to reach. The benefit of the remote sites is the obvious quiet and the fact that on a good day you can enjoy them by yourself and imagine that you have stepped back into time, a time before the area was settled. For me these are favourite destinations and places that I often hike to by myself when I am looking for some solitude.

The following chapters provide information and locations of my top 10 Dundas area waterfalls as well as one in Waterdown that is close enough to include.

These are all within close proximity of each other and so it is very possible to visit some or all in a single day.

Sherman Falls - Ancaster, Ontario

This area is blessed with an abundance of easily accessible waterfalls and Sherman Falls is one that garners much attention.

This waterfall is named after the Sherman family who had a farm in that area. The Shermans are a well-known name in the Hamilton area as Clifton Sherman founded Dofasco Inc. in 1912.

Easy to get to, the trail starts right where Old Ancaster Road meets Lions Club Road in Ancaster. There is parking available on the road there. The trail meanders over reasonably easy terrain for the short distance to the base of these falls. It is somewhat amazing that although it is located just a short hike away from the road and is fairly large in size, many people pass by this hidden treasure without ever knowing of its existence.

A wooden bridge crosses the stream right near the base of the falls and presents a popular vantage point for photo taking.

Sherman Falls is a 17 metre (56 ft) multi-tier waterfall surrounded by rugged limestone, mossy rock and natural forest. It has two cascading drops with a wide flat ledge that divides the upper and lower falls. Water flows here all year.

An easy hike, consider Sherman Falls when looking for a place to day hike or to take striking photos.

Canterbury Falls

Parking at the same location as Sherman Falls (see previous page), the trail meanders up the escarpment and follows the topography of the ridge. In about 15 minutes you will reach Canterbury Falls.

The Canterbury Falls area really has two waterfalls, both of them being fed by a tributary of Sulphur Creek which is also sometimes referred to as Canterbury Creek. Little Canterbury Falls is a 5 metre (16 ft) tall ribbon cascade and is best seen in the spring or after a rain as it can almost completely dry up in the summer months.

The second and larger of the two is Canterbury Falls which is a 9.5 metre (31 ft) high terraced ribbon cascade with a crest width of 3.3 metres (11 ft). It features a wooden footbridge across the creek right at the crest of this waterfall and has water flow all year.

Tiffany Falls. Image by Frances Maas

Tiffany Falls – Ancaster

For a short hike to a beautiful destination, consider Tiffany Falls. This hidden gem is easy to get to and is one of the most picturesque waterfalls in the area.

For me the cascades in the creek and the high rocks that frame the valley make the walk in to the falls very enjoyable. The view continually changes with the seasons.

Tiffany Falls is a 21 metre (70 ft) cascade waterfall and has water flow all year. The best time to view it is in the spring or after a rain when the flow of water increases dramatically.

Tiffany Falls Conservation Area is considered a significant natural area. Its bedrock exposures are considered an Earth Science Area of Regional Significance. The area provides a link between the greenspace corridor along the Niagara Escarpment through the Hamilton urban area and the extensive natural areas of the Dundas Valley.

The forest area is made up of Eastern Hemlock, Sugar Maple, Red Oak, American Beech, White Ash, Basswood, Black Walnut, Hawthorn, Butternut and White Elm.

This area is home to a large number of animals, insects and reptile species as well as many varieties of plant life.

This waterfall is also an interesting one to visit in the winter as it plays host to ice climbing groups. Seeing them challenge the solid ice with their skills and equipment is always fascinating to watch.

Tew's Falls

At 41 metres (134 ft) tall, Tew's Falls is the highest waterfall in the Hamilton area. It is spectacular to see, particularly from below.

The most common viewing point for this waterfall however is from the top level. To get here, drive to Harvest Road in Dundas and look for the signs to the parking area. There is a fee to park here. The trail to the falls lookout is just minutes to walk and there are two viewing platforms from which to observe this waterfall.

See the chapter on the Spencer Gorge for directions on hiking to this waterfall from downstream. Besides the obvious benefit of seeing this spectacular waterfall from the bottom this trail has the added benefit of taking you past Lower Tew's Falls. Although much smaller at only 3.7 metres (12 ft) in height and 6.7 metres (22 ft) in width it more than makes up for its size in overall beauty.

Webster's Falls

Image by John M Goede

Perhaps the most photographed waterfall in the area, Webster's Falls is a short walk from Tew's Falls and can also easily be accessed by car. At 22 metres high (72 ft) and 30 metres (98 ft) wide, the classic plunge waterfall is created as Spencer Creek makes its way into the valley.

There is a parking lot on Fallsview Road with a fee to park. Note that the stairs that formerly allowed visitors to descend to the base of the falls is no longer open to the public due to safety concerns. For hiking tips to get to the base of the falls, please see the chapter on the Spencer Gorge Trail.

Sydenham Falls

Although tucked away and not really marked out well, the three waterfalls that make up the Sydenham Falls area are well worth a visit.

Park at Cascades Park on Livingstone Drive in Dundas. Walking through the park you will see the trail heading up towards the railway tracks and into the natural canyon beyond. The first waterfall you will reach is Lower Sydenham Falls. It is a small cascade and is located directly under the railway bridge. The best way to view it is from an old pedestrian bridge located directly in front of it.

The trail continues under the railway bridge, heading uphill. You will hear Middle Sydenham Falls before you see it. It will be on your right but a steep incline makes getting directly to it difficult unless you have the proper footwear. Be cautious here.

The trail continues and ends at the base of Upper Sydenham Falls. The largest of the three, this waterfall is approximately 14 metres (45 ft) tall.

Dyment Falls - Dundas

Dyment Falls is a complex ribbon falls with several vertical sections. It measures 15.7 metres (51 ft) in height and has a crest width of 4 metres (13 ft).

At the top of Sydenham Road in Dundas there is a lookout with parking. This is a great spot to enjoy the sweeping view that takes in all of Dundas and provides views clear to the lake. Walking a little further up to the top of Sydenham Road you will notice the blue Bruce Trail side trail marker indicating the direction to the waterfall.

The trail begins its descent directly beside Dyment Falls and so provides views at various places along the way. There are rough stone stairs along some of the steeper points and this is a route where you need to watch your footing.

Dyment Falls experiences its strongest flow during seasonal storms and after the snow melts but is impressive at any time of year.

Its source is believed to be a tributary of Spencer Creek which drains the roadside ditches of Sydenham Road and the Dyment farms across the road, hence the name Dyment Falls.

On a return winter visit we had the opportunity to view the falls again, this time enhanced by icicles and frozen sections. Glimpses of water could be seen running behind the ice and along the face of the rock. I always find it incredible that significant sized trees are able to grow and thrive in the steep edges and rocky terrain of the escarpment and there are some very interesting ones to see here.

This waterfall is relatively unknown but is worth the visit. Consider stopping by if visiting the Sydenham falls which are just minutes down the hill. The combination of this waterfall plus the view from the lookout area at the top of Sydenham Road make this a very worthwhile stop.

Borer's Falls

Borer's Falls is a classical 17 metre (56 ft) waterfall and is also known as Rock Chapel Falls. It is considered a true plunge waterfall as the water does not contact the bedrock until it reaches the base of the falls.

The waterfalls once powered the Rock Chapel village sawmill which was owned and operated by the Borer family for over 100 years. Land clearing in the area eventually altered the creek's flow to such an extent that it could no longer provide sufficient energy so the family switched to steam to power the mill.

There are many spots to view the falls including a bridge on Rock Chapel Road that provides a breathtaking view of the gorge.

There is a parking lot at Rock Chapel Conservation Area and the waterfall is just a short walk up the road from this location.

Hermitage Falls

Many people visit the area around the Hermitage Ruins without ever realizing that a very pretty waterfall is just steps away.

Although only 4 metres (13 ft) in height this waterfall is just metres off Sulphur Springs Road and is located directly behind the Hermitage Gatehouse Museum.

To access you can either hike the main loop trail through the valley which runs right past this area or drive to the Hermitage Gatehouse Museum located on Sulphur Springs Road in Ancaster. There is a fee to park at this location.

In any event, walk directly behind the Gatehouse Museum and you will see the waterfall. It is a nice visit in all seasons.

Darnley Cascade

Although not a waterfall in the traditional sense, the Darnley Cascade has an elevation of 4 metres (13 ft). It is formed as Spencer Creek tumbles down from Christie Lake on its way to the former Darnley Mill. It is easily accessed as you walk the Crooks Hollow Historical Trail in Greensville.

Great Falls

Many of the area's waterfalls are relatively easy to access and none of them are more accessible than Great Falls in Waterdown. Travelling by car, drive along the 403 toward Toronto and exit on Hwy 6 North. Turn right on Hwy 5 (Dundas Street East). Head east and turn right on Mill Street. Keep driving until you come to Smokey Hollow Park on the right. You will hear the sound of rushing water immediately as the lookout platform at the crest of this waterfall is literally steps away from the parking lot.

Great Falls is also known as Grindstone Falls and has a height of 10 metres (33 ft) and a crest width of 5 metres (16 ft). Water flow is typically strong here with an increase in water volume noticeable in the spring or immediately following rain.

Don't miss the opportunity to hike the marked Bruce Trail as it leaves here, following a cut trail to the base of the falls and then following the contour of the water as it heads downstream. This area is beautiful and the trail takes you past many rock formations and into a natural setting filled with trees and wildlife.

Historical Areas and Points of Interest

As well containing many areas of natural beauty the Dundas Valley holds within it a rich history. From the time of the early settlers this area was seen as a gem and in fact saw an influx in commerce and homes being established even earlier than most of the Hamilton area.

Remnants of some of this activity remain to this day and can be seen while exploring the trails.

The following chapters explore four of these. The first three are historical sites, each playing a role in the story of the area. The fourth is a much newer spot yet one that plays an important role in the environment stewardship of the region.

All of these are easily accessible and promise an informative and interesting visit.

The Hermitage – Ancaster

One of my favourite areas of the valley to visit in the fall is The Hermitage. This ruin dates back to before 1855 and has a very interesting history. It is particularly picturesque when surrounded by the vibrant colours of autumn.

The Hermitage can be found while hiking from the Dundas Valley Trail Centre and is located on the Main Loop. This trail is a favourite of mine, filled with rolling hills, streams and moss covered rocks. There is a small parking area at the Gatehouse Museum which provides for a shorter trail.

If in this area, step behind the Gatehouse Museum to see the Hermitage Cascade. This beautiful cascade waterfall is 4 metres (13 ft) in height.

From here, enjoy a view of the Hermitage Cascade and then follow the trail as it meanders through the forest and towards the ruins of what was at one time an elegant estate.

According to the historical plaque at the ruins, stones used in construction were quarried from local sites, the red bricks from the Dundas Valley and the limestone sills from the Credit River Valley. The Hermitage had several owners before it was acquired by George Gordon Leith in 1855.

After George's death in 1901 his daughter Alma Dick-Lauder bought the estate from the rest of the family and lived there until 1934 when a fire broke out during a party and burned the house down. Even after this fire Alma continued to live on the site, building a modest home within the ruins where she lived until her death in 1942.

The front facade of the home provides some indication of how majestic it once was. This is an interesting area to visit as you wander around the remaining walls of the house and its outbuildings. A Google search of the site will reveal many articles detailing alleged paranormal activity in this area. One that sticks out was reported by a group of young men who saw an apparition of the house restored to its former glory with lights on in the windows and very obvious signs of life. Others have reported hearing footsteps following them and whispers behind them and someone reported having seen a glowing corpse that vanished when they went in for a better look at it.

The Hermitage history is rich with legend and romantic tragedies of suicide and lovers scorned. The rumours and dark stories of murders and satanic rituals as well as the sightings and quiet woods make it a place that will forever be whispered about when the darkness falls and the moonlight shines. In spite of this, I have to confess that I find the site to be incredibly peaceful, particularly on this fall day.

Sulphur Springs

During the late 1800's the Sulphur Springs Hotel in Ancaster, complete with its mineral spa, was a popular summertime destination. The sulphur waters were believed to have wondrous curative and healing powers and as a result they attracted visitors from far and wide. The hotel closed in 1910 after two significant fires but although the hotel is gone, the fountain that supplied the sulphur water remains.

Stopping the car along the side of Sulphur Springs Road, the first thing you notice is the distinctive sulphur smell. The odour is similar to that of rotten eggs and is difficult to miss. Plaques on the fountain provide some information on its heritage as well as some detail into what makes this water so distinct.

This site is easy to find while driving on Sulphur Springs Road between Ancaster and Dundas and can also be accessed from the Main Loop Trail while hiking in the Dundas Valley. You will find it while hiking the area between the Trail Centre and the Hermitage site.

This is just another unique feature that makes the Dundas Valley such a rich and interesting place to explore.

The Griffin House

Often, when thinking about historical significance in the Dundas Valley our thoughts turn to the interesting history of the Hermitage. Although this is probably the most well-known, there is another important site just a short walk away.

Parking by the Hermitage Gatehouse on Sulphur Springs Road in Ancaster, stop to check out the Hermitage Cascade, a beautiful 4 metres (13 ft) waterfall located directly behind the gatehouse. This pretty waterfall is always worthwhile to see.

Leaving there, head west on Sulphur Springs Road to Mineral Springs Road for the short walk to The Griffin House. Although understated, this site has important historical significance.

Built around 1828, the house sits atop a hill on Mineral Springs Road overlooking the valley. Originally the farm was part of a 200 acre lot granted to David Cummings in 1798. In 1834 it was purchased by Enerals Griffin from George Hogeboom, a local contractor, along with the surrounding 50 acres.

Enerals Griffin and his wife Priscilla had crossed the border in 1829, most likely in the Port Stanley area, to escape slavery in the United States. It is possible that they made use of the Underground Railroad. For the next 150 years their descendants lived and farmed here.

In 1988 the property was sold to the Hamilton Regional Conservation Authority by the estate of the last owner, a descendant of Griffin.

The small one and a half story house is significant both from an architectural and historical point of view. One of the few remaining clapboard homes from the first half of the 19th century in the Ancaster area, it represents a modest working man's farmhouse. Its intact condition with few alterations makes it a noteworthy architectural structure. In addition, the house and site are one of the earliest surviving homesteads in the province.

Archaeologists have unearthed over 3,000 artifacts on this small site including stoneware, porcelain, clay pipes and masonry. Between 1992 and 1994 the house was restored to its early 19th century time period and in 1995 it was officially opened to the public.

This site is managed as a joint project between the Hamilton Conservation Authority and Fieldcote Memorial Park and Museum. It was designated a National Historical Site by the Minister of the Environment, the Honourable John Baird, in 2008.

Standing alone in the shade of this humble yet important structure I tried to imagine what life might have looked like back then. A beautiful piece of history, The Griffin House is an interesting visit.

Urquhart Butterfly Garden

As if the endless trails and waterfalls weren't enough, Dundas is also home to the Urquhart Butterfly Garden. Named after pioneering entomologists Dr. Frederick and Norah Urquhart who after forty years of patient research solved the mystery of the migrating monarchs, construction of Canada's first municipal butterfly garden began in 1994.

Located in Centennial Park on the banks of the Desjardins Canal, it is heavily planted with the varieties of plants needed by butterflies and their caterpillars. It is maintained without the use of pesticides or herbicides, many of which are detrimental to butterfly populations.

The garden now consists of six large raised beds, each approximately 75 × 35 feet, as well as the adjacent bank of the canal. All are planted with shrubs, perennials and annuals.

On any given day as I walk the meandering paths of the garden I will spot a variety of butterflies and other insects as well as song birds. The selection seen depends on the season and so is always changing and interesting. There is a kiosk on site which houses a number of interpretive panels identifying many of the butterflies and plants you will see here, illustrating butterfly metamorphosis and explaining how to create butterfly-friendly yards at home.

According to their website the garden is the brainchild of local businesswoman Joanna Chapman who in 1992 catalyzed the formation of a group known as the "Butterfly Coalition". Members of the Coalition secured funding, identified an appropriate site, solicited contributions in kind from many local businesses and individuals, gained the support of the Town of Dundas and devoted many hours of their own time to planting and maintaining the garden.

Always changing, this area is a quiet and peaceful place to visit.

Exploring by Water

Being at the extreme western edge of Lake Ontario, this region has within it a number of wetlands as well as navigable waterways. In the last number of years, this has become for me a frequent past time. For the birding and wildlife aficionado, travelling via kayak or canoe offers the rare chance to travel into remote spots and with a little luck on your side, the opportunity to get into close proximity to some of the many creatures that call this area home.

Great blue herons and egrets are plentiful as are osprey and numerous waterfowl. The numerous white tail deer, raccoon and foxes can often be spotted along the riverbanks. A highlight can be a bald eagle sighting now that they are successfully reestablishing themselves here.

The next section of the book covers some of the best areas in which to paddle. These are flat water areas and as a result are suitable for paddlers of all skill levels. What they lack in technical difficulty they more than make up for in sheer beauty.

Bring along binoculars and a camera and enjoy yourself.

Desjardins Canal

The Desjardins Canal was originally built between 1827 and 1837. Its purpose was to provide the town of Dundas with access to trade coming by ship via Lake Ontario and to help the town with its goal of being the major commercial hub at the western end of Lake Ontario. Eventually the impact of the railroad eroded the importance of this canal and that plus the growing costs required to keep it maintained, eventually led to the end of its use for commercial purposes.

Now that it has pretty much reverted back to an original state it is a great place to kayak or canoe, particularly in the spring and early summer. Access can be found along Olympic Drive in Dundas. Note that this end of the canal can become weedy and difficult to navigate in the late summer. During that time it can be easier to launch at Cootes Paradise and paddle westward into this area.

Paddling through the canal you soon enter the West Pond, a bulrush and lily pad surrounded section of open water area teeming with large snapping turtles, swans and assorted waterfowl. Crossing this pond you return again to a narrows. At times the water area is barely wider than your kayak paddle with mammoth bulrushes and water grasses pressing in. The song of the red wing blackbirds cajole you along and soon the water opens up again.

Continuing on, you head into the west end of Cootes Paradise which is a terrific area to spot bald eagles and enjoy a beautiful sunset.

The water in the area is shallow, usually just a few feet deep and paddling is easy.

Carroll's Bay

I enjoy paddling through these sleepy little coves. On a summer's day I see dozens of turtles sunning themselves on logs and watch countless fish jumping in the calm water.

Regal looking osprey eye me from their lofty perches and on a couple of occasions fly past me with fish wriggling in their razor sharp talons.

Great blue herons stand as silent sentries along the shoreline or soar lazily overhead while everywhere around me, ducks, geese and swans go about their business seemingly oblivious to my intrusion.

What may be surprising to some is that in spite of being surrounded by all of this natural wonder I haven't even left the city and in fact am only minutes away from downtown Hamilton.

Carroll's Bay is located on the northwest side of Hamilton Harbour at the mouth of Grindstone Creek. The protection and oversight of this area is provided by the Royal Botanical Gardens. Their restorative efforts have been ambitious and have had an immensely positive impact on the return of bald eagles to this area as well as on the protection and sustainment of many other endangered and at risk species.

There is something magical about silently paddling into a protected cove on a calm foggy morning and discovering a couple of sailboats anchored there. Somehow it evokes a simpler time, a time of slower travel and lazier summers.

As I paddle a large group of cormorants glare disapprovingly at me, vulture-like from atop their treetop perch. I leave the water, tired and happy from a great work out and with the feeling that I have discovered yet another great local destination in the Hamilton area.

By water you can access this area via the small parking lot at the bottom of Spring Garden Road in Burlington, just past Woodland Cemetery.

Cootes Paradise

We have some pretty amazing gems right here in our own backyard. From spectacular waterfalls to breathtaking trails, the natural areas around Dundas and Hamilton have lots to offer.

One of the most magnificent of these is Cootes Paradise.

Cootes Paradise is the largest wetland at the western end of Lake Ontario and is on the west side of Hamilton Harbour. It is owned and managed by the Royal

Botanical Gardens and is a National Historic Site, a Nationally Important Bird Area (IBA) and a Nationally Important Reptile and Amphibian Area (IMPARA).

Rising early one morning I launched my kayak at Princess Point and headed around the point and then west behind Cockpit Island and Sassafras Point, exploring the various inlets along the way. The silence was often interrupted by jumping fish and the swans, ducks and geese were plentiful.

On a couple of occasions I was treated to the sight of large blue herons perched in the trees or lazily flying overhead, their massive wingspan reminding me of schoolbook illustrations of ancient pterodactyls.

Crossing over towards Bull's Point I was able to watch numerous waterfowl including some low flying trumpeter swans and mergansers that did low flyby's for my benefit, just skimming the water as they passed.

On prior occasions I have seen the pair of bald eagles that nest along the northern shore but unfortunately not this particular morning.

I enjoyed the sight of water plants and the shoreline, impressed that this level of nature and plentiful wildlife can be found so close to a major city.

I crossed back over heading back towards Princess Point. This area of the bay is one where I often like to pause when kayaking to enjoy the sunset and reflect.

On this morning I simply pushed through and headed back to the dock. I made myself the promise to return again soon to this little bit of paradise in the city.

Christie Lake

With its clean beach, easy access, good fishing and excellent paddling opportunities, Christie Lake is always a worthwhile destination. The entry gate is located at 1000 Hwy 5 in Dundas. There is a fee for entry.

This location offers washroom facilities and safe swimming as well as kayak and canoe rentals.

Paddling the perimeter, particularly late in the season, is terrific and the changing colours of the shoreline trees add to the overall experience.

Home to a large amount of birds, this is a great spot to watch herons as well as ducks and geese. The perimeter hiking trail which takes you completely around the lake is also a very worthwhile walk.

Valens Conservation Area

For a complete outdoors experience, Valens Conservation Area is a good choice. Here you can swim or fish for pike, bass or pan fish. It is an ideal lake for paddling and kayaks and canoes are available for rent.

As well as enjoying the water, Valens also has a complete campground so you are able to stay and enjoy the nights as well.

If you enjoy fishing you have the option of casting from your canoe or kayak plus this lake features casting docks and a bridge from which to try your luck.

In the winter months, when conditions allow it, Valens offers ice fishing.

Valens Conservation area is located north of Dundas at 1691 Waterloo Regional Rd 97, Cambridge.

Final Thoughts

I draw endless inspiration from the trails, waterfalls and countless destinations in the Dundas Valley. It is where I go to think, to reenergize and to gain insight. It is my fortress of solitude, to borrow from a beloved super hero character. Often after spending time wandering beneath its leafy canopy or paddling its area waterways I am driven to capture my thoughts in words. At times I've sat on a creek bank or an elevated meadow and taking in the view with notepad in hand, attempted to capture how it's made me feel. Like a photograph taken of a sunset, my words never do justice to the actual experience or adequately capture it but still, it gives me something to refer back to when I want to remember the day.

It is my hope that through this book I have perhaps provided some knowledge that you can use, piqued your interest to explore something new or if nothing else, inspired you to get outside and explore. Discover your own path, wander a new trail or paddle a new stream. You will always enjoy and will always learn something, perhaps even something new about yourself.

I leave you with a couple short pieces I've written in the field or shortly upon returning. I hope you enjoy them and thank you for sharing this journey with me.

Cam

September in the Valley

Like many, I find the fall to be a special time of the year. Perhaps it is the coolness of the air or the sense that another summer has come to a close but for whatever reason, it has a unique feel.

For me there is no better way to experience it than by walking a quiet trail through the forest. With the unique crunch of fall leaves underfoot punctuated by the sound of the occasional walnut or wild apple working itself loose and hitting the ground it is a treat for the senses. I find that fall even seems to have its own smell, a leafy combination of peppery woods and earth mixed with clean air and what I can only describe as a combination of wet bark, campfires and wool sweaters.

Clearly we as human beings have an ancient and mysterious connection to the land and I really feel it on days like today. Call it an intense feeling of gratitude or an acute sense of appreciation but whatever it is, it is powerful.

The cool breeze combines with the warmth of the dappled sunlight causing an ever changing feel to the temperature that is unique to this time of year. Visually it is a short lived but breathtaking display of intense yellows and oranges mixed with the impossibly fiery reds of the maples and sumac trees.

Walking amongst the ancient walnuts and pines I hear the woodpeckers and the foraging squirrels and am frequently treated to the sight of small groups of deer as they graze, seemingly unconcerned by my presence.

I breathe in the air and am at peace, grounded and content, grateful for another year and for another season on this amazing planet.

Image by Ryan Goede

You Can't Hike the Same Trail Twice

There are a few local trails that have over time become my "go to" destinations when I am feeling the urge to get out for a few hours. These are not necessarily the most spectacular of our local hikes but for me there is a sense of familiarity and comfort on these trails that have made them my place to re-charge, my Fortress of Solitude, so to speak.

In spite of visiting often I am learning that the trail, much like us, is constantly changing, evolving through the changing seasons, growing and dying and never appearing quite the same way twice.

I have also learned that these local and easy to get to destinations can contain within them those same unique experiences and surprise glimpses of wildlife as what we would expect to see in a far more remote area. The lesson here is that a visit to a trail that is close to home can often be as rewarding as one that takes hours of driving and months of planning to get to.

There is room for wonder everywhere as long as you are prepared to open yourself to the opportunity. The changing of the seasons that we experience in our climate play a significant role in this and the sights, sounds and smells on the trail can vary dramatically week to week and, based on changes in the weather, even day to day.

I particularly like to explore immediately after a rain or during a light snowfall. I also find that an early morning hike provides a vastly different feast for your senses than one enjoyed at dusk.

Even a familiar trail approached from an unfamiliar direction makes the experience seem fresh and new.

The Greek philosopher Heraclitus said "No man ever steps in the same river twice, for it's not the same river and he's not the same man."

I believe that this philosophy applies equally to the trail. Because as long as I've opened myself up to being aware, it's not the same. To the uninitiated it may appear to be the same trail but it's still different: different light, different feel, different colours, different sounds, different smells and ultimately a different experience.

I can sense that since my last visit, it has changed, and so have I.

5 Reasons to Get Out Hiking this Winter

At times winter can feel extraordinarily long and cold but even when the mercury plummets, with a little bit of planning, getting out and exploring a trail can be not
only possible but very worthwhile.

Besides the obvious advantage of no bugs here are 5 benefits to getting out hiking in the winter:

Fresh Perspective

Even trails that you frequently explore look different under a fresh layer of snow. Streams and trees look different and waterfalls take on a whole new and spectacular look.

Less People

If peace and solitude are an important component of your hiking experience then winter is the ideal time to get outside. There is something about laying down the first set of boot prints in the snow on a snowy morning that leaves you with a sense of satisfaction, the sense that you are creating a new path.

More Wildlife

The combination of less people on the trails and significantly less leaf cover means you can see further distances. The obvious benefit is that you can spot more wildlife. Deer are easy to find in the valley and woodpeckers and other birds are plentiful. Bring some seed along and some of those friendly birds are likely to get very close in exchange for a snack.

More Exercise

Added winter clothing and snow covered trails add resistance to your movement and with that comes additional health benefits. You can improve your strength and cardiovascular health while at the same time relieving stress and eliminating the winter blues. Hiking is proven to aid in weight loss and helps to protect against heart disease, diabetes and depression. The extra work involved in hiking in the winter burns more calories and provides you with obvious fitness benefits. Staying active and fit during the winter months ensures that you'll be in top shape when the regular season begins.

Improved Mental health

It's been said that it is impossible to be in a bad mood and be in the woods at the same time and I can certainly attest to that. Try walking a trail on a sunny winter day with a light snow falling and you instantly feel the happy effects of endorphins combined with fresh crisp air. Scientific studies have long supported the benefits of nature and hiking on mental health and there is no doubt that it is an effective stress reliever and a great way to clear your mind.

So take advantage this winter. Bundle up and explore. I promise that you will be glad you did.

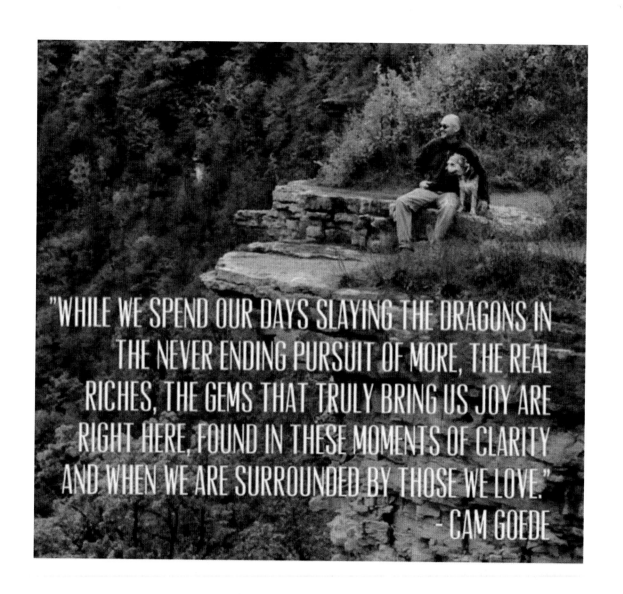

"WHILE WE SPEND OUR DAYS SLAYING THE DRAGONS IN THE NEVER ENDING PURSUIT OF MORE, THE REAL RICHES, THE GEMS THAT TRULY BRING US JOY ARE RIGHT HERE, FOUND IN THESE MOMENTS OF CLARITY AND WHEN WE ARE SURROUNDED BY THOSE WE LOVE."

— CAM GOEDE

Made in the USA
Las Vegas, NV
22 March 2022